Living Life 90 Days At A Time

A Sarcoma Survivor's Journey

by

THOM J. SCHMENK

Featuring an Epilogue by Lee Leddy, MD
of MUSC Hollings Cancer Center

Including a Glossary of Cancer Terminology and Acronyms

ISBN 978-1-68197-541-2 (Paperback)
ISBN 978-1-68197-542-9 (Digital)

Christian Faith Publishing, Inc.
296 Chestnut Street
Meadville, PA 16335
www.christianfaithpublishing.com

Printed in the United States of America

CONTENTS

To Dee.
First you said "Hello."
Then you said "I do."
Then you said "You'll be just fine."
Thank you for saving my life three times.

PREFACE

This writing is presented as a tribute to all those who have and will battle cancer: patients, patients' families, doctors, physician assistants, nurses, technicians, caregivers, and researchers.

In the United States, over 1.5 million new cases of cancer in its more than one hundred different types are diagnosed each year. Over a half million people in this country die each year from the ravages of this disease.

I have tried to share my journey down cancer's path so a newly diagnosed cancer patient may glean some hope from my story. Perhaps a friend or family member will learn herein how to help someone cope with their journey.

It is the hope of this author that this text may raise awareness of this disease and perhaps encourage the reader to support cancer research. Specifically, it is my hope that you will consider supporting sarcoma research. Sarcomas represent just 1 percent of cancers while representing more than 15 percent of childhood cancer.

This text will guide you along the journey I experienced. It is mine and mine alone. Each patient's journey is unique, challenging and personal to each patient. When you complete this brief offering, I hope you feel moved to some sort of action. Be it compassion for a fellow traveler, generosity in your support of research, or perhaps just a better understanding.

Author's Disclaimer

Before we begin this journey together, I want you to understand just a bit of who I am, what I am saying, and how I like to tell a story.

First, I am not now and have never claimed to be a legal professional, a medical professional, an evangelist, or an ethicist. I am not racist or sexist, but my writing is not always PC—politically correct—either. I am just an observer of humankind.

If I give you advice or suggestions, it is because I want you to learn from my experience and be better prepared for yours.

If I tell you that a certain food, product, medicine, or form of exercise is good, it's because it worked for me. Use those examples to form topics to discuss with your doctors and caregivers.

Lastly, before we turn the page, know that if I describe someone as tall or short or thin or fat or black or tan or cute or freckled or funny, it's because I want you to see the people I saw and learn the lessons each of them taught me.

A cancer center's waiting room is a cornucopia of humanity. Cancer patients come in every shape and size. Sarcomas can attack a cute, little five-year-old boy of Japanese heritage just as harshly as it attacked this tired, old white curmudgeon, your author. I found strength in each patient I met, and I hope you find some in the pages to follow.

ACKNOWLEDGMENTS

If I tried to thank everyone who accompanied me on this journey, this acknowledgement would be longer than the actual text. My first thanks and my eternal love and gratitude go to my wife, Judy. I would not have made it through life, this journey, or this book without her. Thank you, Team Positive. You know who you are and how important you are to me. You were there for the journey. I hope you appreciate this humble narrative

I am unable to completely express the extent of my gratitude to my physicians, Lee Leddy, MD, of Charleston's Medical University of South Carolina (MUSC) Department of Orthopaedics and Jennifer Harper, MD, radiologist at MUSC's Hollings Cancer Center and all the other doctors who assisted with my care. My thanks also go out to Physician Assistant Barret Willis, MUSC's nursing staff, and all the associated technicians.

Lastly, my thanks go to my friend and my editor-in-chief Shirley Berardo for her encouragement and for her skills as a wordsmith.

Thom Schmenk
Sarcoma Survivor

INTRODUCTION

Cancer isn't just a physical malady. It's also an emotional journey for which no one can prepare you. No one. I watched cancer enter the lives of those around me from my youngest days. It seems like, in some way, it has always been around.

I was born in 1950 and was fortunate to grow up in a small post-war, blue-collar neighborhood in Euclid, Ohio. Lucky for me, our house was just a few houses away from Edgecliff Drive that ran parallel to the Lake Erie shore for miles.

One of the earliest birthday gifts I can remember was my twenty-inch Roadmaster bicycle, training wheels and all. The sidewalks of my street provided the training grounds, and once I learned how to ride without training wheels. I was always riding my bike. I would imagine some great journey riding along Edgecliff, perhaps slaying a dragon or two down on the beach.

The older I grew, so did the size of my bicycle and the distances I could travel.

I owned a bike my entire childhood and kept my last one even after I got my first driver's license.

Along with my childhood dreams and adventures, there was reality as well. Cancer affected my family far too soon. Cancer is a journey that begins when it pounces upon your loved one, relative, or friend. It continues as you watch from afar as famous people share their stories. Newspaper obituaries are punctuated with the disease whose name often goes unmentioned. Some days my bike rides would be clouded by the memories of those who left this life too soon after battling ever so many different types of cancer.

Cancer first seized my attention watching a maternal uncle be consumed by skin cancer. In the 1950s, cancer treatment was not as powerful as it is today, and many journeys were cut too short, too soon. My cousin, a Korean War veteran, would leave us too early fighting liver cancer. A beloved elementary school teacher wasted away before her heavy-hearted students as breast cancer devoured her in just one school year.

How fortunate I am that five-plus decades later cancer research and advances in cancer treatment would help save my life.

It has taken a while to place my journey on these pages. A journey of days filled with uncertainty, then action; fear, then hope; tears dried by love; pain treated with laughter; then finally joy, true joy. But cancer is a cloud that follows you, lurking behind like a thunderstorm flashing in your rearview mirror. Sometimes you are forced to look back over your shoulder just to see if it's coming back.

I was fortunate to marry my high school sweetheart at the young age of twenty-one.

As newlyweds we bought a tandem bicycle and rode the paths of my youth along the lake shore. A year later our firstborn son, Todd, joined our lives, and we would move to Concord Township, Ohio, in 1972. Our youngest son, Thad, came along in 1974. That was the same year I joined the fire service as a volunteer firefighter with the Concord Township Fire Department.

Then in 1977, I was fortunate to join the Lyndhurst Fire Department for a thirteen-year career as a firefighter/paramedic. Working on the ambulance and in the emergency room, one learns how precious and fragile life can be. It was good to be part of a team helping people on a daily basis.

In 1990, I took an early retirement from the fire service, and we moved to South Carolina. My next career soon followed as I stayed close to public service working in risk management and the insurance fields.

In 2004, I watched a colleague allow himself to be turned into a virtual guinea pig as researchers used trial programs to try and save him from pancreatic cancer. A year later my father-in-law waited too long to discover kidney cancer and fought like John Wayne to stay viable and with his loving family. Two stronger, braver men I have never met.

Cancer tests you. It makes you search for strength and hope. It knocks you down, then lets you back up and lingers waiting to see how much fight you have remaining.

Truth be told, fight, strength, and hope are floundering seeds inside each of us. They hide, dormant until awakened by a challenge, watered by tears and nurtured by those around you who share their love and support with you on your journey.

At age sixty-two, in 2012, I retired and bought a new ten-speed bike to start my second childhood. How ironic that I retire, focus on health and fitness, and a year later, cancer would be my diagnosis too.

I was encouraged to write and describe my experience with cancer by two brave cancer journeymen you will meet in later chapters. I wrote *Living Life 90 Days at a Time: A Sarcoma Survivor's Journey* to share what I learned along the way and to offer hope to those beginning their own journey. The "90 Days at a Time" part is because even when you survive the fight, your doctors maintain a vigilance to help you guard against cancer's sinister reoccurrence.

So come with me as I climb onto my ten-speed bike and wonder, "Where do I go from here?"

Chapter One

Where the Journey Began

Bike riding is a bit like life, the harder you pedal
the sooner you get there. Hopefully the breeze
will keep you cool along the way.
—Thom Schmenk

Stationary bikes never held much interest for me. I spent most of my life working in government, and my job just before I retired was strikingly similar to stationary cycling: pedaling like crazy and going nowhere.

I always admired my father-in-law. He was the consummate career police officer and proud father of my wife and two younger siblings. My favorite story of his was how as a rookie he brought home a Christmas tree in the trunk of his patrol car. So, in October of 2012, on the day before I retired, I brought home a ten-speed bike in the trunk of my work car. It was a good way of celebrating my retirement and remembering Jack at the same time.

Biking returned to my retired life as a casual hobby, just an occasional ride around the fifty-five-plus retirement neighborhood we moved to earlier in 2012. It was nice, just enjoying a leisurely pace, calmly riding without a care until some older-than-me neighbor would back his car out into my path and remind me of my mortality!

Within just a couple of months, biking became an obsession. I bought a safety vest, helmet, flashing safety lights, and rearview mirror. I had it all tricked out like some kid. Then I began venturing outside of our neighborhood, onto the main streets of our development. Over time, the ride grew from a mile per day to five or six miles per day, four or five days a week. My weight started to drop. I slept better. Even my family doctor was impressed. Hey, retirement may be as good as some say after all. Plus, I'm healthier now than ever before—or so I thought.

As I got off the bike one day, I noticed an odd, egg-shaped lump on the inside of my left thigh. *Gee, what's that? Hmmmm, doesn't hurt to touch it. Guess I must have bumped it or something, maybe a pulled muscle. Have to keep an eye on that,* I thought.

Little did I know, a new ride began.

CHAPTER TWO

Delay in Diagnosis: Mistakes Happen

Mistakes are the portals of discovery.
>   —James Joyce

Weeks passed, and my newfound leg lump wouldn't. So where would you go for medical advice? I went to the bike shop! Yes, indeed, off I went with my bike in the back of my (personal) car to see the wizard of all on the planet—the bicycle repair guy! (See above quote.)

Upon entering the bike shop, I was greeted by an energetic, young midtwenties sort of man. I explained my thinking that I needed a new bicycle seat. Of course, the wizard of cycles inquired as to why I felt so.

I quickly showed him this rather curious, now slightly larger-sized lump on the inside of my left hamstring and proceeded to explain it must be from the seat. He quickly questioned that if the seat was the root of my evils, why then was there not another lump on my right leg. Curses, I was foiled by youthful logic! Even so, I persisted in my belief (hope) that it was from the seat.

The young wizard was obliging and kind to this old fool. He showed me some affordable options and convinced me to try a ladies-size conventionally shaped seat that was tapered with a hole to allow air to pass through it. He installed it for me and had me try it before allowing me to leave his emporium.

Off I went determined that this new twenty-first century, high-tech tapered seat of the future would solve my dilemma. Actually, I wondered why I settled for an old-fashioned girl's bicycle seat, but I digress.

I went riding my bike that very day and explored my new retirement community with a quickened pace and a renewed sense of purpose, sure that my problem would soon shrink away as the ice in my tea does in the summer.

Alas, the ice in my tea continued to melt each day, but my newfound dilemma did not. At this point, my loving wife ended her silence and demanded I go see a doctor about the lump, and if I didn't make the appointment, then she would.

I met my wife, Judy, on my seventeenth birthday. She walked into my party, and as the saying goes, she had me at hello. As I've admitted countless times, the dress she had on made me notice her even as she walked away. She became the love of my life. We were married just four years later as I watched the scowl on my father-in-law's face melt to a smile as he gave me her hand.

We've been married at this writing now for forty-five years. We were still children ourselves when our first son, Todd, was born in 1972. Our youngest son, Thad, came along in 1974. The four of us sort of all grew up together.

Judy has been my partner in so many ways; she is my best friend, a lover, the mother of our children, my business partner, and my biggest critic while always my biggest fan.

I introduce her here because her actions from here on forward probably saved my life! I will live the rest of my years being reminded of that, but it is true nonetheless. At her "encouragement," I made an appointment, and what transpires here forward is proof that having an advocate in your corner is crucial to navigating the turbulent waters of health care.

My family practice doctor examined my leg with great care and a bit of puzzlement. He admitted never quite having seen anything quite like this odd-shaped possible hematoma. He asked if I had any idea as to the origin of this nasty-looking beast. I shared my bicycle seat theory. He said that if it was sports related, then we should treat it like one, and prescribed applying ice daily for one week. I explained that I had already tried that after seeing the bike shop wizard and it had no effect, positive or negative. So he asked me to try warm, wet compresses and come back and see him in a week. It took just the first two days to realize that was not the answer. The lump didn't like heat. It became nasty, grew in size, and now displayed ugly red and blue veining all over its surface.

I reported this new finding to my doctor by email, and he prescribed an immediate ultrasound test which was done the following week. The ultrasound tech admitted to never having seen anything like this and said she thought the doctor was looking for a possible DVT, or deep vein thrombosis. A large blood clot to you and me!

Another week passed before my doctor said the ultrasound didn't show anything; he was sure it was not any form of lymphoma and proceeded to throw up his hands and refer me to an orthopedist. He assured me this orthopedist was his friend and had treated his mother. *Great*, I thought, *now this young doctor is placating me as he would his parents.*

Now we were weeks into this investigation and still no answers. Maybe I didn't want an answer. I surely didn't want the answer I eventually got. I can't blame "the system" for all the delays; I've been pretty laid back so far.

On the first visit, the ortho doc looked at the ultrasound film and said it was a waste. He said x-rays wouldn't show what he needed. He poked, pushed, prodded, and then said it was time for an MRI.

More days passed as I found my way through insurance pre-approvals and appointment clerks to the MRI clinic. Two different staffers made sure that I was wearing nothing—absolutely nothing but what they provided, a drafty hospital gown—and that any and all of my earthly possessions were now locked in a locker. All I had was a one-size-fits-all gown and a plastic key on a plastic string for my locker. Staff guided me to hang my key on a wooden pin just outside the MRI room door as I entered the true all-knowing wizard's den. This was it. This would tell us what's going on.

Chapter Three

The MRI Tells All

I'm going to get an MRI to find out whether I have claustrophobia.

—Steven Wright

I've had my share of injuries as a firefighter, so I was not a complete stranger to an MRI. My first one was back in the stone age of medical imaging, 1989. As I recall, the tube they placed you in was incredibly, awfully small. I remember lying down on a table that was then electronically propelled backward as you went in head first. I cringed as my shoulders bumped the side walls of the tube and I was ordered to "scrunch a little for me, darling" as this sugar-plum fairy of a technician instructed me to relax and breathe slowly.

When the table stopped moving, I opened my eyes. The dimmest of all night lights ever invented barely illuminated my tiny space, and I realized the top surface of the tube was just inches from my nose. The only saving grace was the quiet hum of a small fan that moved just enough air past my face to assure me that perhaps I would not suffocate before the end of the test. So this experience prepared me for what was to come some twenty-four years later.

Flash forward to 2013, this afternoon, the technician brought me to the MRI room where for some reason the machine did not look quite as imposing or as small as I recalled. Then she instructed me to recline on the table with my feet pointed toward the opening. She informed me that because of where the lump was that I would be going into the tube feet first and that my head would rest at the edge of the opening. A small consolation, but when the table stopped moving, I was able to see just a bit of the room lighting if I tilted my head and looked back. This time, they provided me with headphones that she said would help me relax. I even got to select the music, so I asked for and they were able to play Johnny Mathis!

A calming voice came on over the intercom and asked me to please remain very still during the test and that I may be able to hear some loud banging noises during the test and not to be alarmed. Suddenly, loudly, the beeping, honking, banging noise was so loud I couldn't hear a word Johnny was singing. Oh well, it's the thought that counts.

The test lasted longer than I thought. The table was moved back and forth several times and Little Miss Calm Voice finally whispered that the test was complete. Johnny was still singing, but all I wanted was to get up and out of there.

After I got dressed and reloaded my pockets of all my worldly treasures, I was ushered toward a door to the lobby area. Right then and there it began. Right then and there I knew for the first time I might be in some serious trouble.

I've spent enough time around emergency rooms, hospitals, and doctor's offices to recognize that look. It was the "I'm going to remain emotionless and inform you to see your doctor immediately" look. The MRI tech looked at me and said, "Normally we just give our patients one DVD of their test, but here's three. You may need an extra one and always make sure to keep the third copy for yourself. Good-bye, sir, and best of luck to you."

It hit me. It hit me before I reached for my car door handle. I knew I was in for a ride.

Chapter Four

Waiting and Worrying

Pray, hope and don't worry
—Saint Pio of Pietrelcina

Some sixty more hours would pass before our next appointment with the orthopedist. Sixty hours to worry, wonder, jump to the worst conclusions, and then worst of all, we couldn't resist the temptation. We put the DVD into our home computer.

The computer buzzed and whirred and spun the DVD. Finally, the screen filled with a license agreement and the instructions to download the DVD viewer. Oh, come on! Really?

More time passed. The download finished, and up jumped hundreds of individual images that all looked like a leg muscle from dozens of different angles.

Out of sheer frustration, I scoured my brain for what to do next. I could not find any instructions that would say how to use the viewer. I could see something, but what?

I remembered that a neighbor was a retired surgeon and his wife a retired nurse. I frantically called them and told them my story. I pleaded with them to come take a look at these images, and they came immediately.

He explained he was a retired surgeon—an oral surgeon. We pulled up the images, and he did his best to interpret this bundle of graytone images before us. He assured me what I thought was a tumor was actually the image of the cross section of the femur, the longest and strongest bone in your leg, actually in your entire skeleton.

Absent the instructions of how to run the viewer, we were limited, but he did point out what showed to be an egg-shaped mass on the side of the hamstring, but without knowing how to run the viewer, we could not figure out how to see it in more detail.

On a side note, if we would have simply used the scroll dial on the computer's mouse, it would have controlled the magnification, and we would have been able to close in on the image better.

In retrospect, it was probably a good thing we didn't do that. Actually, the only thing worse than doing this was looking up my diagnosis on the Internet, but we will discuss that bad decision later.

At some point that evening I remembered the quote at the top of the page. "Pray, hope, and don't worry." We prayed, we hoped, but we still worried.

CHAPTER FIVE

Bad News Isn't Wine. It Doesn't Improve with Age

Bad news isn't wine. It doesn't improve with age.
—Colin Powell

We entered the orthopedist's office a few days later and waited, waited, waited.

After allowing enough time for our collective blood pressures to rise, for our palms to sweat, and for all conversation between us to stop, we were taken back to an exam room. The doctor entered a short while later. At least I think it was short. By then neither my wife nor I had much of a sense for time.

The doctor took the DVD, placed it into the computer. It was then I learned how to navigate the images, but by then what did it matter? He studied the images extensively, removed his reading glasses, and said, "Sir, you are in some serious trouble here. This appears to be a large sarcoma. There is only one man in Charleston, South Carolina, who can save your life. Fortunately, he is a friend of mine. I will have my nurse set up a referral appointment for you. Wait here."

"Wait here." "Wait here." And he upped and walked out of the room! We were numb, confused, full of questions, and this guy got up and left us cold by ourselves in this closet-sized, freezing-cold exam room.

So we waited and waited and waited until we couldn't stand any more. My wife finally opened the door and asked, what now? Was the doctor coming back? The nurse explained that the orthopedist could not do anything for us, so he moved on to other patients. We could go now, and someone would be in touch with our referral appointment information.

All I remember is the next thing we were sitting in our car in the parking lot, looking at each other, and wondering what the hell just happened. It was the Friday of the week before Thanksgiving Day 2013, and we didn't know what this holiday season held for us.

This was when my wife became my lifesaver. This was where she became "Super Advocate" and took action, immediate action! "You stay here, just stay here," and before I could speak she bolted out of the car, leaving her purse behind on the front seat of the car. She never leaves her purse, not anywhere!

I'm not good left alone. Left alone I do foolish things. So just to be consistent, I did my next foolish thing, I Googled the word sarcoma.

Sarcoma

> sar·co·ma (sär ˈkōmə/) noun
> a malignant tumor of connective or other nonepithelial tissue.

Bad move. Why did I do that? Oh shit! Malignant? Oh shit!

As I looked up, Judy was approaching the car like a humming-bird racing toward me. When she got in the car, she said, "Here. Here is the name of the doctor at MUSC. His name is Dr. Lee Leddy. They said he is the best and the only one in Charleston who knows how to take sarcomas out of extremities. They said he's the only one in town who can save your life. We need to call his office—now."

She reached into her purse, got out her smartphone, and dialed the number.

We were transferred once or twice, but we were finally connected to Monica, Dr. Leddy's coordinator. Judy explained our situation, shared what little we knew, and asked for help.

Keep in mind, this was the Friday of the week prior to the Thanksgiving Day holiday. Monica said, "I can't get you in Monday, but be on the seventh floor of Rutledge Tower at 8:00a. m. on Tuesday. We will find a way to work you in. Bring a book or something to do. You may be here a while."

Judy and I hugged, and this was the very first time she looked at me and said, "You're going to be fine, just fine." I've heard those words from her a million times, and then I heard those exact same words from three other amazing people along my journey. They were right!

It started right there and then. Her positive attitude never wavered. (If it did, she never let me see it.) Judy became the first member of what would come to be called Team Positive.

CHAPTER SIX

Advocacy: You Need Someone At Your Side and On Your Side

To make a difference in people's lives through advocacy and through supporting research— that's the kind of privilege that few people will get.

—Michael J Fox

> **Advocate,** *noun.*
>
> *1. One that argues for a cause; a supporter; a defender.*
> *2. One that pleads in another's behalf.*

In life we all need an advocate. An advocate is your champion, your protector, an encouraging voice along the way. They may be your spouse, your best friend, your sibling, or your pastor.

Whether you are a newly diagnosed patient or the family member or friend of a cancer patient, an advocate is the most important person on your journey along the path cancer will lead you.

My wife, Judy, was my first and best advocate. She demanded the referral information on day one. She made the call to get us to the next step of our journey. Those two steps alone may have saved my life! She is always there to ask the tough questions, to demand answers, to question why, to pester, to cajole, and to get whatever we need to keep our travel as smooth as possible.

You need an advocate, a friend a C-Buddy to go along on your visits to the doctor. It's a good idea for them to have a notebook and pen to write down what questions you have for the doctor and make sure those questions get answered. So, too, it's equally important to write down the answers for you so you can recall them later. Some days you will be too tired or too worried or too sick to remember what you were told, so it's good to have someone there who can pay attention for you.

To Cancer Patients

The first thing cancer does is to take away your control. You have to listen to the doctors. Your journey is now in their hands. I can't tell you how many times I whined, "I want my life back!" It's frustrating. It becomes hard to keep track because your journey feels so out of your control. But there is no need to travel this road alone. Select someone who can make you laugh, talk about the good times, and share funny stories. Your "advocate" can be your spouse, significant other, best friend, oldest friend, newest friend, or coworker.

Often, another cancer survivor will step forward and share their story and offer to be your treatment companion. They've been there. They make great advocates. Don't be so proud as to shun their offer. Occasionally, you can drive yourself to and from a radiation treatment. Sometimes it's good to be alone, but often, it's best to have someone be with you.

Advocates come in all shapes and sizes. I was so blessed and fortunate to have support from my wife, sons, family members, and friends. There were so many advocates; I named them Team Positive. They called once in a while. A few stopped by just to hang out, play cards, or watch a movie, but most, most simply checked in by e-mail. They e-mailed a funny picture; they just said hello, how are you, and they really wanted to know. They emailed a joke or cartoon. Some shared a cancer success story they knew or saw in the news. Some quietly offered their thoughts and prayers. Most importantly, they let me know they were there. They were just there, and sometimes that feels so comforting.

To Family or Friends of a Cancer Patient

Over the course of my journey, I watched as many friends and neighbors were stunned by my diagnosis. Each one had a different reaction of their own, and you know what? I had to learn that was okay! One neighbor of mine suddenly became very quiet. They pulled away, and I recognized they were worried and didn't know what to do or say. Some family members were scared for me, worried about me, but still didn't know what to do.

So here's an easy recommendation for what you can do: All you have to do is just be there. You don't need magic words. You don't need gifts. Most often, all you need to do is just be there.

My oldest son, Todd, and my daughter-in-law Beth traveled from out of state during my radiation treatments. After being there for a day, Beth said it best. "We decided just to show up and see how you were. We waited to see how much you were willing to share, and then we just listened, simple as that."

The Best and Worst Things Said to Me

Best: "Your news is just f——ing awful."
"Cancer really sucks, but I'm right here for ya man."
"We're gonna fight through this thing together."
"Hey, you look great... but I'm a lousy liar too."

Absolute worst: "I know just how you feel."(No one knows exactly how you feel! A cancer survivor can tell you they remember how they felt because you're both there. But no one else knows just how you feel! *Please, don't ever say that to a cancer patient.*)

Worse: "Oh, I knew someone who died from that!" (Gee, thanks, I feel so much better now!)

The best thing you can do when a friend or family member is fighting a major health issue is simply just to be there. Let them know you're there to listen. Let them know you care. Put up with them when they're angry. Pray with them. Pray for them. Cry with them when it's scary and help them laugh, often. Laughter feels great, even when it hurts.

CHAPTER SEVEN

A Medical Team That Cares Can Save Your Life

Life is a journey. When we stop, things don't go right.

—Pope Francis

The journey continued Tuesday morning before Thanksgiving Day. Today, there would be bumps in the road, no road blocks, but big bumps.

As we were told the Friday before, we arrived on the seventh floor of Rutledge Tower, Department of Orthopaedics, before 8:00a. m. We nervously checked in and took a seat in the waiting room. Amazingly soon, a wonderful nurse, Chris, walked out and asked us to come with her. We followed, and she did the usual first-time intake information gathering, vital signs, etc. She made us as comfortable as possible and guided us to a large exam room and explained the doctor and his assistant would be in, but it may be a short while. "Short while"—that's a medical term for "open a magazine and relax."

I stared at the exam table covered by the usual white paper roll, but I opted to sit in a chair right next to Judy. We sat close, up against each other, always in touch. She played solitaire on her phone. I think I tried to read the news on mine. We were out of things to say. We just tried to breathe and not let go of each other. Sometimes denial is the only place to hide.

The room door opened, and for the first time we met Barrett Willis, Dr. Leddy's physician assistant. She had a genuine smile and introduced herself calmly. She said that she, Dr. Leddy, and some other physicians were reviewing the films, and they would be with us "in a short while."

I imagined we were seated at the Stuttgart Hauptbahnh of waiting for our train, looking at the faded, old arrow-shaped signs pointing toward Budapest, Vienna, Berlin, and Paris. It's amazing how your mind can create a comfortable place to go when you're really, really nervous. When denial doesn't work, then dream!

The door opened once again, and in walked PA Barrett and Dr. Lee Leddy. Dr. Leddy was very tall with scattered blonde hair and a boyish smile. I remember thinking how old I must be because the doctors and the police officers all looked younger than my own two sons. Dr. Leddy introduced himself and asked Judy and I to slide our chairs over close to the exam table. He sat on one of those round, horrid stainless-steel doctor seats on wheels at the end of the table. Again, I could sense this wasn't going to be good. I could tell because PA Barrett moved back and leaned on the wall near the door. She probably saw the look on my face, and I guessed it was her job to stop me if I tried to run.

The good doctor confirmed what we already knew. My lump was very likely a sarcoma, but they would need a biopsy to confirm. He let that sink in for a minute, and I suddenly felt a different lump in my throat and hoped he would continue before I choked on it.

He took out his pen, pulled down the white paper that covered the exam table, and used it like a football coach designing the next play. He explained the next step was to do some tests and find out exactly what type of sarcoma this was. He said that in most cases lumps like this located in the soft tissue of a limb don't kill people. It's only a cancer that spreads that is lethal. (Well, that's one smiley face on the board for me!) Then he went on to lay out three options for treatment. (Frowny-face time.) He said worst-case scenario would be that there was more cancer elsewhere in the body. If that were the case, then his colleagues at Hollings Cancer Center would take over from there. He said we would do a whole body CT later to be sure. The next possibility would be to lose the entire left leg, followed by chemotherapy. The third possibility would be to treat the sarcoma with a radiation program followed by surgery to remove the sarcoma along with a safe surrounding margin and save the leg. (Back to one-half smiley face.)

Dr. Leddy then said he wanted to start with a biopsy. I sort of saw that one coming and expected a horse-sized needle that he would go in and pull out an ounce of flesh to test. Wrong again. The doctor explained he wanted to do a series of biopsies along the gracilis muscle to gather enough tissue to get a good diagnosis. Okay, time to drop the drawers and let him and the PA take a look. After some considerable, less than enjoyable, and slightly awkward groping, he said it was time for me to recline on the table and let's get started. I realized I hadn't looked at Judy for a few moments and noticed her pale face and expression that said it was time for her to step outside. I kissed her and said to ignore the screaming and to follow close behind me if I made a break for the elevator. She smiled as best she could, and the good nurse Chris walked her out to a chair in the hall.

Recline does not exactly describe the position I wound up in. My posture resembled that frog we all dissected in high school biology class. The doctor then produced this gun-like device that looked like he was going hunting for small game, scientific game perhaps, but a gun-like device for sure. He explained that the gun made two clicks. The first was the spring being set; the second would inject and remove the needle in two quick steps. I should prepare myself on the first click because the second would be a bit of a punch.

Ow! SHIT! What was that? Apparently, I didn't hear the first click and, POW, the first biopsy was done. Fortunately, I think I yelled loud enough to cover the huge fart that escaped when the first needle hit. (All things considered, farting and yelling were better than some other possible reactions.)

Okay, so now I'm ready; let's do the next one. I don't think I ever heard the first of any of the clicks, but I didn't react as badly as I did for the first. He said he wanted to do a couple more, and we continued. Around number three or four he managed to strike a nerve. I mean he literally stuck the needle in and hit whatever nerve descends through that area of the thigh muscle. When I lurched and yelled, I said it felt like a nerve conductivity test I had once.

All in all, we did ten or eleven biopsies that day. Geographically, they started somewhere parallel to my left testicle and traveled down the leg to just above the knee. Judy came back in to the room, and they explained that I was done and that the doctor would call with the results as soon as he could, but he cautioned that it was a holiday week and the labs were over loaded, so it may take a few days.

As I went to get down off the exam table, I suddenly felt like I was either going to faint or puke or both. Nurse Chris got me seated in a chair and gave me a bucket and a damp cloth for my forehead. Judy sat with me, hoping I didn't do either.

The good doctor and PA had used a good part of their morning schedule for me, and I knew I had just probably made them run late for the balance of their day. So now, for the past two years, when I go there for a follow-up appointment and they say he's running late, I don't complain. We read or watch TV or get a snack in the lunch room because we know he probably helped another new patient that day.

CHAPTER EIGHT

Waiting and Worrying II:
The Journey Starts Uphill

What, me worry?

—Alfred E. Neumann

Somehow we found our way home that afternoon, and I applied ice to nine or ten puncture wounds, which were quickly becoming small hematomas. My leg looked like I had been attacked by a rabid woodpecker, but this would at least get us some answers.

The next morning we were exhausted from the day before and all the tossing and turning that night. We then realized Thanksgiving Day was tomorrow and we had a house to clean, a table to set, and preparations for our youngest son, our daughter-in-law, and the three grandchildren.

I started to think of what to say tomorrow. "Hi, happy Thanksgiving! Guess what, I have cancer." No that won't do. "Hey, happy Turkey Day. This turkey has cancer." No, that won't do either. Besides spoiling the holiday, it would create hundreds of questions, and we had no answers. None.

Tomorrow was Thanksgiving Day. It would be time to put on a happy face and suck it up already! This wasn't a return trip to denial. It was the only way to have a happy Thanksgiving. Then it started the questions in my mind. Is this my last Thanksgiving Day? How sick am I already? When are they going to call? Again, Judy's strength got us through another day. Yes, I am most thankful for her. If this journey is on a ten-speed bike, it's a tandem bike for sure.

By late Wednesday afternoon, we couldn't stand it anymore. We called and reached PA Barrett. We anxiously asked if they knew anything. She was calm, reassuring, but had no answers. She explained the test cultures take time and they could not make a specific diagnosis without allowing proper time. She assured me the doctor would call—on Friday. Great, just great, this turkey day is going to be a real challenge.

The holiday arrived, and all I can remember of that Thanksgiving Day (or all I'm willing to recall) is when I said the Thanksgiving blessing. I remember thinking, *Lord, thanks for a wonderful life, but where do I go from here?* We were glad to be surrounded by family, and the day passed quietly as we spent another day in denial waiting for the phone to ring.

We drew a line at noon on Friday. This time Judy called, but Barrett's answer was the same. I don't know how Barrett does it; she has to deal with worried, panicked people all the time and maintain her composure. She promised we would hear as soon as they had complete results.

Suddenly, loudly my iPhone began to play a smooth jazz ringtone. The caller ID said "No Caller ID." but we knew who it was, all right. (I deleted that ringtone shortly thereafter. The song it came from still gives me the chills when I hear it.)

"Hello, Thom, this is Dr. Leddy." I can't recall exactly what I said, but he continued, "I wish I had better news, but we waited for all the results to come back to be sure, and it's a leiomyosarcoma." I grabbed a pen and asked him to spell it so I would get it right. He told me he wanted to meet with us first thing Monday morning as this was not something that could wait another day and that he would have a plan ready for us by then. The call ended. I looked up at Judy and said, "It's cancer. It's a leiomyosarcoma, and he wants to see us Monday morning."

I admit it. I lost it. Totally freakin' lost it. I don't know how many times I whined, "Oh shit!" It was the only thing I could say. Brilliant, huh? Just over and over again. I ran to the bedroom, grabbed my pillow, sat on the edge of the bed, and repeated it over and over. Totally selfish. Totally out of control. Poor Judy gave me some space, then came and sat next to me, and we hugged and cried. I think we cried the rest of the evening and well into the night.

The next two days were a teary-eyed blur, but I recall talking to my best buddy, Steve. He and his wife, Candice, knew we were waiting, and they called to check on us. We sobbed over the speaker phone and told them our news. Then after they hung up, we ran to the medical dictionary and, worse, to the Internet. Big mistake! (Hey, at least I was consistent. I did it again like the day in the car.) Don't ever, ever Google your diagnosis. At least not until your doctor has had a chance to really help you understand where you are.

A while later, Steve and Candice called back. Steve is originally from Scotland, so imagine hearing his distinct accent say, "Eh, Thom, we just looked this up on the Internet. Have you seen this? This is major stuff you're dealing with!" (Great minds think alike, eh?)

Somehow, we survived the weekend, and the sun still rose Monday morning. It was time for the next drive downtown. The valet parking guys at Rutledge Tower are great. They are the first ones to greet you upon arrival, and they have no idea what's wrong. They just do what they can to make you worry about one less thing.

Up to the seventh floor, check in and back to the waiting area. Fortunately Nurse Chris spotted us and brought us back to the exam room quickly. We didn't wait long today; in walked Dr. Leddy and PA Barrett. They smiled, and you could see the confidence on their faces and in their demeanor. "I've consulted with several people since we last spoke. We have a plan. I think we can beat this, and I think we can save the leg. We need to do a head to toe CT to be sure before we start, but here's the plan."

Dr. Leddy was sending us to Dr. Jennifer Harper, a radiologist, and she would do a six-week plan of treatment. Then some rest would be in order. Then they would surgically remove the sarcoma. The doctor explained the plan in detail—his reasons for the plan, a description of what would take place—and then he openly reviewed all the side effects and the things that could go wrong. He assured us we were going to beat this, and off we went to make an appointment to see Dr. Harper at Hollings Cancer Center.

CHAPTER NINE

The Healing Power of Faith

Faith sees best in the dark.
> —Vice President Joe Biden, para-
> phrasing Kierkegaard

The National Institute of Health's National Cancer Institute reports that religion and spirituality are important to cancer patients.

> Many patients with cancer rely on spiritual or religious beliefs and practices to help them cope with their disease. This is called spiritual coping. Many caregivers also rely on spiritual coping. Each person may have different spiritual needs, depending on cultural and religious traditions. (NCI, NIH)

One's faith, religion, or spirituality is an individual decision. To some, it's the dominant controlling force in their life. Others have lesser degrees; some don't have any. It's unique, personal, private, and powerful.

My religious foundation was set in the guilt-laden, judgmental environment that was the Catholic Church of the 1950s and '60s. Fortunately for me, I had a maternal uncle who was a Catholic priest, a "hippie priest" of the '60s. Father Frank taught me that religion and faith are personal and, most importantly, that all people are on God's highway, they are just in different lanes. I was taught my faith and to respect those whose faith was different than mine.

A cancer diagnosis can shake your faith or, in my case, strengthen it. Like many from my generation, my participation in the church had an ebb and flow to it, drifting away, slowly returning. I've never been a very good evangelist; however, this diagnosis got me to back to church on Sundays for sure.

As any guilt-laden Catholic, I entered the confessional booth one Saturday afternoon, having prepared myself to confess my sins and ask for God's forgiveness. I knew not what lay ahead on this journey, but how could I ask God for strength along the way without asking Him for his mercy first?

This brings me to the introduction of the first of three angels that I truly believe God sent me along this journey. No, I'm not talking about tall, winged creatures in long, glowing robes and certainly not the three who visited Ebenezer Scrooge on Christmas Eve. Each of my angels were black, two were older men, one a pretty young lady. All three were strangers, totally unexpected, and they all carried the same message, but like old Ebenezer, I never realized it until the third.

When I entered the confessional, I bypassed the safety of the kneeler behind the room divider and found myself sitting face to face, knee to knee with the priest. I raised my head and saw Father Tim. I discovered later that he was originally from Nigeria sent to live in America just shortly before we met. He had the warmest eyes and a calming, peaceful smile. I cannot and will not share what transpired initially between us, but I will share that at the completion of my confession there was joy, welcoming, and celebration. I watched as a huge smile came over Father Tim's face as he welcomed me back to our Father's house. Gone were the admonitions of guilt! No fire and brimstone, just warm prayers for my return and for my journey ahead. At the end, as I stood to leave, Father Tim reached out, smiled, and placed his hands on my shoulders and calmly, confidently said, "You are going to be fine. Just fine, I know this."

As I left the confessional, I drew the usual looks of concern from some others waiting in line. I took so long in there they probably thought I just confessed to being a serial killer! I tried to drum up an old-fashioned Catholic-guilt expression on my face, but all I could do was smile.

All along my journey friends and family sometimes offered to add me to their prayer list. I never turned anyone down. I didn't care what religious denomination they might be; the more voices raised above on my behalf, the better. Early on, I was warmly and carefully approached by the husband of my wife's boss. He explained being very active at their Jewish temple and wanted to know if it would be all right to add me to their prayer list. I smiled, admired his compassion, and shared my Uncle Frank's story about God's highway. I think that by the time my surgery rolled around, I was on at least one prayer list of every denomination!

CHAPTER TEN

Treatment Plan Set Then Angels Arrive

A day without laughter is a day wasted.
—Charlie Chaplin

Dr. Leddy had reviewed the tests, completed his plan, met with his colleagues, and they all concurred. He explained that the sarcoma research done at MUSC and other institutions was conclusive. They considered doing surgery first, then following it with chemo and radiation treatments. Instead they had decided that we would do six weeks of radiation, then a few weeks of rest to allow the surface skin to heal, then return to him, and they would surgically remove the sarcoma. He assured me they were now "*my* team of doctors," and they all agreed.

He then explained all the possible side effects. The radiation would be projected through two sides of my thigh. The surface skin will most likely be damaged. There will be lotions for the skin allowing time prior to surgery for the skin to heal, but there could be infections or post-surgery fibrosis. Also, he warned of the possibility of a second surgery if the tissue was so damaged that when they closed the incision the skin might not heal the first time around.

The positive part of the plan was that the radiation would kill or sterilize the sarcoma; however, they did not expect to shrink it. They would then surgically remove the sarcoma along with a safe margin around it. If all went well, that would be it. No follow-up radiation or chemo. Recovery would be slow—months not weeks. Physical therapy was a possibility, and there would be a small residual "dent" in my leg. A residual dent in my leg, is that it? Are you kidding? Do I look like the type who still wears a Speedo at the beach? Hey, who cares? Let's get this next part of the journey started.

This trip was to Hollings Cancer Center in Mount Pleasant— another waiting room, another friendly nurse, another exam room. This day we would meet Dr. Jennifer Harper. Her reputation was stellar. Dr. Leddy trusted her implicitly, and I never heard a negative comment about her.

The exam room door opened, and in walked Dr. Harper, accompanied by another resident doctor. As she extended her hand, I saw a tiny, young, unassuming woman with a disarming smile and an air of confidence that made my wife and I both relax, instantly. She spoke directly in detail, but in words and terms we could understand. She explained the part of our journey that she would now direct.

Next came a trip to Hollings downtown. (I was allowed to go this one alone!) I had to meet with Dr. Harper and two (thankfully male) attendants who would design the target for the radiation and apply the first of my marking "tattoos." I explained in an earlier chapter that "my lump" was on the inside of my left thigh. Let's just say perpendicular to my left testicle. I provide you with this tidbit so you may understand my obvious concern about having a beam of high-powered radiation penetrate my left thigh only after beaming very closely past the family jewels.

I donned yet another fashionable hospital gown and contorted myself into a frog-like position that would align with the radiation equipment. Fortunately, these two young men had a sense of humor that matched my own. They assured me they would keep "the boys" out of harm's way. (May I have an Amen?) After the measuring and targeting session, it became time to take a test x-ray of the site to ensure accuracy.

This is where it gets even funnier. These two kind masters of radiation technology began to take small linen towels and surgical tape and create a sort of sideways sling designed to pull "the boys" to one side and tape them in place. The only problem was the tape crossed some various sensitive strands of hair. Hair that would later wage a considerable protest as the tape was removed! We tried several different ways. They even took a picture of the final arrangement so the actual technicians who would do the daily treatments could duplicate their design. Confident in their design and plotting, the next trip was back to Mt. Pleasant for my first treatment.

Dr. Harper met with us that morning and introduced Mary Ann, the chief radiologic technician. She would be the one to lock me into place each day so that the radiation would be precise and exact. Did you catch that gender-specific pronoun? *She* would be in charge, and her assistants Brie, Autumn, Lisa, and Beth were all also ladies. Looking back, they were always kind and very professional, and their expertise eased an awkward situation for us all.

MaryAnn directed me to a changing room where it was back into another stylish gown. Into a large, cold treatment room I was greeted by the telltale hum of the radiation machine. They played music in the room each day, but that hum was ever present.

Mary Ann and her assistant guided me into position, and this being the first treatment, Dr. Harper was right there too—all working to guarantee a precise dose of radiation directed at just the right spot. Then it became time to "sling the boys." To break the ice a bit, I commented that it took until I was sixty-three years old to have three women all working to move "the boys" around. Not knowing when to quit joking, I explained that while I had no plans for procreating, I wasn't done using them just yet.

If you find yourself in for radiation treatment, do not make jokes on the first day! These ladies take their work very seriously! Their sense of humor surfaced after a few visits—just not on the first day. They worked and they taped. I think they enjoyed taking off the tape just a little too much!

A day or two later, MaryAnn said, "Listen, this ain't gonna work. Are you a briefs or boxers guy?" I said boxers and was then instructed to wear briefs the next day. "Wear briefs, and we'll just have you twist 'em to the right side. Yes, that will work much better—unless you like the tape, in which case we can stay with the sling." It was payback time, and I watched a wry smile spread across her wise, freckled face. Five days a week for six weeks. Same drive there, same five-minute procedure, same drive home. No pain, no discomfort, just precise medical treatment.

Each day, when the technicians left the room and the machine began beaming its humming ray, I silently screamed at the cancer. "Die," I said, "die, you cancer. "You lose. I win. I can feel you shrinking, losing, and dying." Prayer is important, but I learned from so many other cancer survivors the power of positive thinking, positive imaging. I silently screamed at that sarcoma every day, every treatment.

This was the place where I met the second of my angels.

I begin by saying that the folks at MUSC are all very compassionate, all very good at what they do. They are also extremely protective of a patient's privacy. Signs abound everywhere reminding patients of HIPAA, the Health Insurance Portability and Accountability Act, which requires they maintain patient privacy.

However, when you are among a crowd of patients all sitting in the chemo/radiation waiting room of Hollings Cancer Center, is there any doubt as to why we're here? Come on, the guy next to me isn't here because he has a social disease. The nice lady sitting across from me with her knitting isn't here to teach mitten making! After a while you pick up on what rather resembles a jailhouse mentality. "Hey, hi, what're you here for?" Sometimes if you ask another patient, "How are you?" you may get no reply, or maybe, you won't get a word in edgewise afterwards.

In my case, I began to see a pattern at the Mt. Pleasant radiation waiting area. Some folks were there every day; some every other day. It depends on your treatment. You quickly learn the routine: Check in, have a seat, a technician greets you, go to a changing room, put on your gown, and wait to be taken to the treatment room. Then reverse the process and go home.

One patient in particular caught my attention. He was a tall, black man with a huge presence. He had strong, piercing brown eyes and a handshake that could crush a tree. He looked like a retired football player that life had hunched over. He was quiet and moved slowly. His dark, sullen face still wore a friendly smile. He was often the patient called just before me each day, and I began to try and speak with him once in a while. It started with "Good morning" and grew to "Hey, how ya doin'?" and other low-key banter. One day, as he was walking out and I was walking in, I teased him saying, "Hey, did ya warm up that table? I hate it when I sit down and it's ice cold." He replied simply with a wise, friendly smile.

Some days I watched as he drove in and parked his gold-colored Cadillac Eldorado in one of the handicap spaces. The patient crowd grew bigger over time, and once in a while we got to talk. He said he was fighting lung cancer for the second time, and of course, there was me and my "lump."

One morning near the end of my treatment plan, I was having a bad day, and he recognized I was feeling sorry for myself. For some reason he and another patient were called back before me, so when Mary Ann came to get me from the waiting room, my large friend had dressed and was walking out. I moped as I crossed the room and saw him walking straight toward me. When we met in the middle of the room, he placed his hands on my shoulders, smiled, and said, "Man, you're gonna be just fine. I know this." I didn't realize exactly what he said until I was in the changing room. I said the prayer to Saint Peregrine as always while there, went to the treatment room, silently screamed at the sarcoma, and the day went on.

The next day he was not there, nor the next. I inquired with the nurse as to what happened and got the standard HIPAA excuse that they couldn't talk about other patients. Now hold on a minute. When you complete your last treatment, all the staff members gather around and you get to ring a huge ship's bell that is mounted on the wall. It's a celebration, your release from the halls of treatment!

I never heard any bells last week, so Monday I persisted—no, I insisted they tell me what happened to my friend. Did he transfer downtown? Did he die? Was he ill? Come on now! The nurse relented and asked me to describe my friend. We had never introduced ourselves to each other, so I described my large friend, even his car. The nurse insisted they didn't have anyone like that; she was sure.

I never saw my large, dark, well-worn friend again. I have yet to figure it all out. This was either the best example of maintaining patient privacy or perhaps I was losing my mind! Or was it divine intervention? Whatever it all was, Angel Number Two had delivered the same message as number one, but I still didn't see the connection.

The treatments continued, and so did my journey.

CHAPTER ELEVEN

Team Positive, Good Friends, More Angels

A real friend is one who walks in when the rest of
the world walks out.

—Walter Winchell

Six more weeks of the journey had passed. Thirty consecutive
radiation treatments completed. The only days off were Saturdays,
Sundays, Christmas Day, and New Year's Day. Add in two extra days
off for the horrible ice storm that locked down Charleston that winter. They were added back on at the end.

I was fortunate, blessed once again. Although I was warned and
given skin lotion to help, my surface skin damage was hardly noticeable for the first three weeks. Then, I awoke in the early morning one
day. My leg was on fire! I threw back the bed sheets expecting flames
to greet me. Instead, what I saw was the brightest, reddest skin I had
ever seen.

Now, I've always been a blonde-haired, blue-eyed, pale-skin sort
of white guy. You know the kind who has to get out in the sun just
to neutralize the blue. Most summers my choices were pale white or
red-faced burnt!

For the rest of the time from here to the surgery in March, I would apply bottles of special skin lotion to all the skin from the top of my leg to the knee. It helped at first. However, by the end of the treatment plan just the brush of my pant leg against that area reminded me this part of the journey would be challenging.

If you have radiation and they give you skin lotion, apply it right away. Don't wait for the "sunburn" to show up. Then it's too late. And make sure you ask for a new bottle on Fridays. Running out of lotion on Sunday night is not a lot of fun.

The doctors said I needed time to let the skin heal. It was the beginning of the New Year, and I needed to rest. Keep applying lotion to the area and hope the area heals well soon so we can do the surgery without surface tissue complications. Take some time off, follow up with Dr. Leddy in February.

It was cool and damp in South Carolina that winter, and the last thing we wanted was to sit and stare at each other for two months, wondering what this New Year would unveil. This was when more advocates, more friends stepped forward.

My wife was still working full time. Her boss could not have been more supportive. She told us we needed to get out of town for a while and worked out a plan to allow Judy the needed time off. We decided Florida was much warmer and a good place to crawl back into some healthy denial for a while.

For more than the last thirty-odd years we had been fortunate to share our lives with Chris and Dan and their three children. We raised our collective five children together and early on began the tradition of spending New Year's Eve together most every year.

Somehow the tradition was maintained. Even though we moved from Ohio to South Carolina, the kids went off to college, and then they retired to Florida, we strived to keep it going. We missed New Year's together this year because the treatment plan ran late, but we headed for beautiful Holiday, Florida, soon thereafter.

It was a great time but an awkward time as well. I slept in the guest room. The bed was small. I tossed and turned most nights. Judy slept on the sofa in their den. I paced most of the day, as sitting down was hot and uncomfortable and walking around created a most needed breeze.

We stayed for days without getting thrown out. We toured, we shopped, played card games, and told our favorite stories from the past. My mood vacillated to say the least. Looking back, I'm lucky they all didn't conspire to feed me to the gators somewhere in a nearby swamp. It bears repeating; I'm not a very good patient.

After nearly overstaying our welcome, we drove across Alligator Alley to Fort Lauderdale. Judy once again passed up an opportunity to throw me to the gators along the way. We finally arrived at my brother-in-law Jack's beachfront condo tower on a beautiful Florida day. The kind of day the Florida Tourist Bureau boasts.

I found a wonderful place to hide! His condo featured a small, breezy balcony with a view of the beach to the right and the Intracoastal Waterway to the left. I could sit and let the breeze cool my leg. I watched the planes fly overhead as the tourists came and went, but most of all I could sit and pray—prayers of thanks for getting me this far, prayers that asked for more strength to continue this journey. Did I mention the view? The view was wonderful!

Jack was quick to spot me feeling sorry for myself and could see the tension and worry in his sister. "On your feet, you two, let me show you the beach." Moments later we toured the building's many amenities and found ourselves on a huge, beautiful patio overlooking the Atlantic Ocean and a gorgeous white sandy beach.

As we began to walk along the beach, I took a picture of Judy and Jack together, and then Jack took one of Judy and me with the ocean in the background. It was one of those annoying moments when thoughts like "Is this the last picture of us together?" creep into your mind. It was time to hold hands, stay close, walk, smell the salty ocean spray, listen to the waves, and enjoy the moment.

Suddenly Judy said, "Hey, look!" She lurched forward and picked up a large piece of coral that was on the beach among the shells. She was looking for sand dollars, but this thing was the size of a small football. We rinsed it off in the surf and discovered it was in the shape of a heart! It was January, but we found our valentine to each other there on the beach.

CHAPTER TWELVE

Footprints in the Sand

We are each of us angels with only one wing, and
we can only fly by embracing one another.
                            —Luciano De Crescenzo

Today it was time for our final pre-op meeting with Dr. Leddy.
Another drive to Rutledge Tower, another smiling valet parking
attendant, in the door, and another elevator ride to the seventh floor,
we arrived. Having gone through all the stages of emotions, we had
now arrived at acceptance. It was time.

It was late in the afternoon on the Thursday before next week's
surgery day, Wednesday, March 5. We stared out the tall windows
and watched as a thunderstorm washed in off the ocean and soaked
the commuters driving across the Ravenel Bridge.

Ortho was backed up. We waited until after 4:00p.m. to see
Dr. Leddy. We reviewed the procedure together. He demonstrated
where he anticipated the incision would be. He described his plan
to remove the sarcoma intact and a healthy margin all around. He
detailed admissions, pre-op, the surgery, recovery, and possibly going
home as early as Saturday.

He reviewed the chart one last time and realized we had never
had the pre-surgical lab tests. He said we should go downstairs imme-

diately. Barrett would call and set it up. It was almost 5:00p.m., but the lab stayed open until 5:30p.m.

We said our thanks and good-byes for the day and that we would see them next Wednesday. We didn't say we looked forward to seeing them; why begin to lie this late in the process?

We exited the elevator on the first floor and made our way toward laboratory services. We were headed up the hall while a great many employees were headed out the door to join the masses into rush hour traffic, away from Charleston's peninsula and home to the Low Country's suburbs.

We found the lab and were directed to their registration office. Judy was tired and waited out in the reception area off the main hallway. I entered the office where I would meet the last of my three angels.

Waiting in the registration cubicles was a pretty, black, young lady with a warm smile on her face. She explained she would only take a minute and then she would walk me back to the lab. As I took my seat, my eye was caught by a montage of words and colors that decorated the one sidewall of her tiny cubicle. Pinned there for all to see was a collection of prayers and artwork depicting some of her favorite devotions.

As I've mentioned before, one of the first lessons of this journey was realizing there is no such thing as coincidence. As a reinforcement of that lesson, I quickly noticed that in the center of this display was *my* most favorite prayer!

My eyes went quickly to a gold poster showing the soft sands of a beach with two sets of footprints traveling the poster's margins. It was no surprise to see that the prayer was Footprints in the Sand.

FOOTPRINTS IN THE SAND

One night I dreamed I was walking
along the beach with the Lord.
Many scenes from my life flashed
across the sky. In each scene I
noticed footprints in the sand.
Sometimes there were two sets of
footprints, other times there was one
only. This bothered me because I
noticed that during the low periods of
my life, when I was suffering from
anguish, sorrow or defeat,
I could see only one set of footprints,
so I said to the Lord,
"You promised me Lord,
that if I followed you, you would walk
with me always. But I have noticed
that during the most trying periods of
my life there has only been one set of
footprints in the sand.
Why, when I needed you most, have
you not been there for me?"
The Lord replied,
"The years when you have seen only
one set of footprints,
my child, is when I carried you."

A chill washed over me. It was as if a Charleston sea breeze had just gently passed through an open window. I explained that Footprints is a favorite of mine. I had a copy of it inside my locker door during my career as a firefighter. At this point in my journey, there was only one set of prints on the sand, and they weren't mine.

She spoke of being raised as a Catholic in New York and that she had changed to the Methodist Church since moving to Charleston a couple years ago. I shared my uncle's highway theory, and she smiled and agreed.

She then escorted me back to the lab where the only remaining technician greeted us by saying, "Oh, look, this one's worried. A big guy like you is afraid of a little old needle?" I explained this was the last step prior to my surgery and that her needle was the least of my worries just now. We laughed together as my blood seemed to take forever as it slowly drained into the test tubes. The technician said, "Come on now, honey. I get to go home today too." The blood-letting complete, the tech walked me back toward the lobby.

As I rounded the corner, the young lady from registration was standing looking out through the glass door to the lobby with her back toward me. She must have heard us approach as she quickly spun and walked directly into me. Embarrassed, I apologized and thanked her again for sharing her "wall" with me.

For the third time in my journey it happened! She looked directly at me, placed her hands on my shoulders, and said, "You're going to be fine, just fine. I'm sure of it."

As I walked into the lobby, it hit me! I realized that the same message had been given to me, identically, three times by three totally unrelated people. "You're going to be just fine." Judy echoed this same feeling to me daily, but these three strangers all said the same thing without knowing their connection to the others. As we headed for the door, I felt that chilled breeze again and hoped and prayed they were right.

I have played these three messengers' stories over and over in my mind a thousand times. I never asked God for a sign of any kind. All I ever prayed for was the strength to get through the journey. Yet he sent me three beautiful, strong, inspiring people.

Have I already told you? I don't believe in coincidences anymore!

CHAPTER THIRTEEN

Treatment Complete: Today Is Surgery Day

You beat cancer by how you live, why you live, and in the manner in which you live.

—Stuart Scott

Buzzzzzzz. Buzzzzzzzzz. The alarm went off that morning at 4:30a.m. I was awake, just lying there trying not to disturb Judy, but I knew full well she was awake too. D-day—or in our case, S-Day, Surgery Day—had arrived. We needed to be there by 6:00a.m.

The drive downtown was easy this morning. We were just ahead of the morning rush. Candice called to say Steve was on his way down. He would keep Judy company and wanted to be there when the surgery was done. Candice said she would be there after work.

We parked our car in front of MUSC's Guest House. We had made reservations for Judy to stay there for two nights after the surgery. The Guest House is located across the street from the MUSC Horseshoe. We walked across the street silently, holding hands as we went.

The only people around were this morning's other surgical patients, so we followed them, all of us lost and nervous looking for the surgical registration desk.

"Good morning, sir, name please? There were all the usual questions, sign here, sign there, a lesson for Judy about the electronic board in the waiting room and how she could track my progress through surgery and into the recovery room. Lastly, I was awarded my prized MUSC patient ID wrist bracelet. We were directed to a huge waiting area and told a nurse would come for me shortly. We entered the waiting room, and I saw no visible signs of security guards. Apparently, they didn't care if anyone ran away from here.

We sat and talked about going home on Saturday, and Judy assured me I would be fine one more time. A tiny nurse called my name from the other end of the room. We said "I love you" to each other and walked toward her.

"Okay, Mr. Schmenk, welcome to pre-op. Please take everything off, place all your belongings in the bag, put on this gown, and make yourself comfortable under the sheets." Comfortable, are you kidding? It was my last chance to bolt, but I didn't remember the way out. The nurse asked Judy to return to the waiting room and said she could come back once I was settled in. Settled in, are you kidding?

Nurses came in and busied themselves with all their usual duties. One connected the EKG lines. Another sized up my veins and started the IV lines. Another reviewed my history and told me the anesthesiologist would be in shortly. Everyone checked my little ID bracelet every time just to be sure I hadn't escaped and hired a surrogate to take the hit for me.

Judy was allowed to return, and we held hands. There were few words; we traded love by osmosis now. Different nurses and doctors all dressed in their surgical scrubs stopped in and checked on us frequently. It was too late to run now. I was attached to too many wires and tubes! We waited together for the surgical techs to come and get me amid all the hustle and bustle. We didn't have much left to say; we just tried to breathe and waited. It was a nervous, quiet scene.

Finally, two young interns arrived and said it was nearly time to go. "Okay, you two, time to play kissy face. We're gonna give you some happy medicine, and we'll be off in a minute." These two guys enjoyed their job way too much! Judy and I hugged and kissed. She told me I would be fine one more time, and I assured her I would do my best to be a good patient, but she knew better.

One of the interns stepped over and injected something into the one IV line and said, "Okay, it's time to go, sir." Judy and I exchanged one more "I love you," and off I went. I remember expressing my concern to the interns that when I had my gallbladder removed years ago I was awake enough to watch the surgeons counting instruments when we entered the surgical room. The interns laughed and said, "See those doors up ahead? You'll be asleep before we get there."

I said, "Oh, really? Well . . . *ZZZZZZZZZZZZZZZZZZZ ZZZZZZZZZ!* "

What followed was a brilliant example of the expertise of Dr. Leddy and his surgical team. During a three-hour-long procedure, they made a seven-inch incision along the inside of my left thigh. They had to be careful, as the tissue they were cutting though was damaged from all the radiation. They informed me several times prior to the surgery that there might be difficulty getting the incision to heal afterwards due to potential infection, resistance to closing, healing, and later, fibrosis. They warned of a possibility of a second surgery to get the incision to properly close. Lastly, I knew there would be a drain line coming out of the leg after the surgery.

Anatomically speaking, they were able to keep the sarcoma surrounded and contained as they removed a portion of the medial hamstring along with significant portions of the gracilis muscle. They maintained clean margins and successfully removed the sarcoma.

The lab tests would later show that their treatment plan had worked. The radiation had rendered the sarcoma 95 percent sterile and only remaining 5 percent of cancerous tissue.

The surgeons finished by actually performing a second surgery to remove any damaged tissue and reshape the area around the incision to allow the best chance of healing and provide shape and support for the remaining medial thigh muscle structure.

Zzz, snort, um, uh, oh.

I opened my eyes and awoke in a complete haze. "Well, hello there, welcome back," a smiling nurse said as she checked all the numbers and lights next to my bed. I said, "When are we getting started? Why am I still here?"(I'm positively brilliant on drugs. Eh?)

"Oh my, you're all done, dear. You're in recovery, and we're going to take real good care of you. You gave us quite a time there. We've had a hard time making you comfortable, but I'm glad you're awake now."

Ow! Shit! I moved my left leg for the first time, and it felt like I just ripped it open. Note to self: *Let's not do that again.* Yawn. I asked whether my wife could come back, and the nurse said they wanted to make sure I was comfortable first. Here we go again. *Comfortable, are you kidding?*

My second act after returning to the conscious state was all male, yes, typically male. I thrust my right hand under the sheets and, damn, there it was. They had put a urine catheter in prior to surgery, but fortunately as I had requested, after I was asleep. I was more anxious and worried about that damn catheter than I was about the surgery—well, almost. I groggily recalled that what goes in must come out!

Judy then appeared through the curtains and smiled and said, "See, I told you everything would be okay. You're fine. And leave that thing alone. You're fine." I brought my hand above the sheets, and we hugged for a long, long time. She was so warm, and she smelled so, so good. Tears of relief filled both our eyes, and I fell back asleep again. When I resurfaced, Judy said she had seen Dr. Leddy, and everything was fine and that he would see me tomorrow.

A new nurse came through the curtain and introduced herself and said she would be my nurse for this shift. (This poor lady is numbered among so many whose names escape me). One thing I will say is Judy and I both noticed that she looked just like Katie Lowes, the actress who portrays Quinn on the TV show *Scandal*. It's funny the things you notice when you're tired and bored.

Turns out that this nurse was as smart and kind as she was attractive! (Darn, she's young, smart and attractive and stuck with caring for old, ugly me.) She brought ice chips, got a chair for Judy, and checked on us frequently. She explained we may be together for a while as the tenth-floor rooms were all full, and she cautioned again that I may stay in recovery for a while.

Later, she checked the catheter along with its holding bag and decided my urine output was sufficient. I knew what was coming next. My facial expression said it all as I began to squirm like any man-child would. "Oh, I swear, the bigger they are, the more you men fuss." She looked at Judy and said, "Look at him fuss, and I haven't even started to do anything yet." I silently appreciated the fact she did not point and laugh, and then I recalled some good advice I had received from a member of my Team Positive. "When they come to take out the catheter, take in a real deep breath. Then, as they pull it out, let the breath out like you were blowing up a balloon. By the time you're out of air, it will all be over." I followed the advice, and it worked. I believe my hand dove back under the sheets to make sure everything else was still there, and my attractive new friend left in disgust. Judy just shook her head and said "Well, that's over now, and (All together now) *you're just fine!*"

The next thing I discovered was the large dressing over the surgical incision. Its proper name is an incisional wound VAC. It is a large dressing that provided a vacuum-like seal over the wound for maximum infection prevention. It achieved its vacuum-like hold because the entire perimeter of the bandage was a very sticky tape. This margin held like a cross between packaging tape and duct tape. In fact, I gave the resident doctor assisting Dr. Leddy the nickname of Dr. Duct Tape.

The main problem with this device was that they applied it quickly, completely covering the incision. But if you recall, this incision was very near a very special area, and this super sticky margin was applied over the edge of the pubic hairs on the left side, near the top of the incision. So as if the incision wasn't painful enough, every time I moved, the tape would tug on those little, terribly sensitive ends. I finally figured out something had to give, so I gently slid the pinkie finger of my left hand along the edge and under those few little captured hairs. One, two, three. YEOWWW! It was rather like pulling off a Band-Aid, but this time the tape held and the hairs gave way. One uncomfortable moment was better than feeling those pull every time I moved.

Time passed, and other patients arrived and were cared for in the other curtain-bound recovery stations. Judy's cell phone rang, and she stepped out to the waiting area to take the call. When she returned, three people came with her. I was so glad to see our friends Steve and Candice. I was not, however, as pleased to meet a nice young lady who said she was from PT, physical therapy.

PT, pull and twist, pain and torture, physical terrorists, your friends and mine. I will never forget her opening line. "Hi there. I'm from PT, and it's my job to get you up for a little walk." *Are you kidding me? Really? Now? I just got "comfortable."* I could think of a thousand reasons for her to leave me alone, but I knew none would sway her determination. A walker magically appeared at the bedside as she threw back the covers. My wires and lines were gathered together, and she said, "Okay, let's start by sitting up and swinging our legs over the side of the bed."

I thought, *Our legs? The only legs "swinging" here are mine!* I believe that at this point some of my more flowery language from my firehouse past may have surfaced. I'm going to blame the medication for my language and my lack of recall of those details.

I saw a look of horror on Candice's face as she saw the look of pain on mine. She mercifully grabbed Judy and said they were leaving to get Judy something for dinner. Gee, thanks, Candy, have a drink for me!

Steve stayed with me and used that smiling wit of his to tell me to suck it up and get it done. He and PT lady got my feet on the ground and my hands on the walker. I was scared of somehow splitting wide open or, worse, falling down. A belt was placed around my waist, and Steve supported me from behind. (I doubt he enjoyed that view!) With their combined assistance, I took my little walk and made it back to bed. Again, the lack of recall is kinder than the actual memory.

Judy and Candice returned from dinner, but no one brought me anything. (Gee, thanks, guys. I'll just have some more ice chips!) Yawn. I awoke later. Steve and Candice had left, and Judy was in a chair with her head resting on the side of the bed. There were still no open beds on the tenth floor, and the nurse from the night shift said I'd be here until morning. Judy and I kissed goodnight (she still smelled so warm, so good), and a security guard escorted her across the street to the MUSC Guest House.

The night passed slowly. I had a view of a wall clock through the opening in my curtain, and the night just dragged. There were a few other patients "on hold" waiting to be admitted to a floor room. We were kept awake most of the night by other patients brought in after emergency surgeries. I remember one patient was a gunshot victim whose family surrounded his bed and argued about whose fault it was. When I finally had enough, I screamed for them to take it outside. A nurse escorted them out. The night shift staff then corralled all the patients waiting for rooms to the far end of the recovery room, and I couldn't see the clock any longer.

CHAPTER FOURTEEN

Rest, Recovery, and a Ghost Arrives

A wise man should consider that health is the
greatest of human blessings, and learn how by his
own thought to derive benefit from his illnesses.
—Hippocrates

Judy awoke the next morning in the warm surroundings of
a cozy room at the MUSC Guest House. She took some pictures
of the room with her smartphone so I could see the historic charm
of old-fashioned Charleston décor. She dressed and made her way
across the street and found me, still in a bed in the recovery room.

"What are you still doin' here?" she said as she parted the curtains. She kissed me hello (How does she always smell so good?), and
I could see in her eyes she didn't sleep much more than I had. Just
then, our pretty, actress-look-alike day nurse arrived for her shift and
was surprised to see us still in recovery. She sprang into action and
moved us into an isolation room in a more private corner of recovery.
She said we both might get some rest here. Kindness in action!

Our kind nurse returned with a menu and instructed us both
to order breakfast and it would be delivered to us there. She also
became concerned that the anesthesia had apparently locked down
my GI tract and said I needed to drink a lot and I had better "go"
before too long!

Rest did not come easy, as we no sooner shut our eyes and our nurse was back with the news that there was a room open on the tenth floor. The overhead fluorescents flashed like strobe lights as we exited the elevator, and I was rolled into a room on 10 where we met a new nursing staff and explored my new surroundings.

A while later, our breakfast order lost in transition, Judy set out on a quest for breakfast. (Some folks need their coffee, but Judy without a Coke Zero in the morning is not something you want ever to see). It was a good thing, because as she walked out of the room, Dr. Leddy's resident, the dreaded Dr. Duct Tape, entered. It was time to change the incision bandage. (Remember what I said earlier about the catheter? What goes in must come out? Well, what goes on must come off!) "Okay, sir, it's time to change this. There isn't an easy way. There are four sides. How about we go long, short, long, short?"

I knew what was coming and tried taking in a deep breath and letting it out as the procedure went on. Zzzzipp. Didn't work! Yeoww! Doggone! Okay, go ahead. Get it done already! Zzzzippp. Zzzzippp. Zzzzippp.

He finally crumpled up the old bandage in his gloved hands, and I watched as it landed in the nearby wastebasket. He inspected the incision and said, "Dr. Leddy did great work." He said (everybody now, all together), "It looked fine!"

Before I could say anything, he opened the cover on a new VAC dressing and applied it so quickly I just cringed. "Geez, Doc! You caught all sorts of hair again here! You gotta pay attention before you slap that thing on!" He almost apologized for his speedy technique, but this time he produced a small pair of bandage scissors to trim the trapped hairs and set them free from the pulling "duct tape" edges.

Our youngest son, Thad, arrived just before dinner time. He felt obliged to take his mother to dinner. (Geez, again? Did you bring your old man a burger or anything?)

When they returned, Thad played the much needed role of family comedian and entertained his mother and me. I'm afraid that by then I was not a good audience.

The abdominal pressure had now reached "uncomfortable," and I knew the nurse would solve the problem soon—mechanically!

I could handle the enema, but I was scared shitless (pun intended!) that it would be accompanied by reinserting a urine catheter. I was not a happy camper.

The evening drew late, and I suggested that my son walk his mother over to the Guest House, and I would deal with what else this night would bring. Sure enough, in walked the nurse with the enema bottle, but thankfully, nothing else. The anesthesia finally loosened its grip, and I was horribly sick the next twelve hours.

To skip the details, the rest of the night can be summed up in the phrase "Clean up on aisle 3!" In between projectile vomit and exploding bed pans, all I did was apologize to the nursing staff. So here is the payback I promised them.

The nursing staff on the tenth floor west at MUSC's hospital is the largest collection of saints anywhere. They never once complained or made me feel worse than I already did. I can only imagine them drawing straws at the nurses' station to see who would answer each time I called. They held my hand. They gave me cool towels to wipe my face. They were far more than just there! Thank God for nurses!

The night droned on like the noise of a squeaky old storm shutter blowing in the wind. The explosions eventually lessened. Early Saturday morning, Dr. Duct Tape arrived for one last bandage change. I was too tired to fuss. I don't think he enjoyed the air quality in the room as he changed the dressing, and I managed to keep all the tiny hairs out of harm's way.

A short while later Dr. Leddy arrived. I told him that his henchman Dr. Duct Tape had already done his dirty work, changing the dressing. He explained that's why he has residents to assist him and flashed a smile that was both wise and droll. He inspected the leg and said the surgery had gone well. I asked if he had seen the sarcoma. He replied that he had not seen it yet! "What? Didn't *you* remove it?" He went on to explain that they managed to keep the sarcoma totally encapsulated in soft tissue along with a clean margin and that he would not see it until they began to examine it in the lab next week.

Dr. Leddy explained that the dressing would stay as well as the drain line and canister until I saw him on Monday. It was Saturday morning, and he kept his promise of sending me home. The only caveat was that I would have to demonstrate to PT that I could get out of bed and move around with the use of a walker. For once, I would be glad to see the PT lady!

Later in the morning, Judy walked in and asked why the room door was closed. "Oh my God, now I know why it's closed!" and she spun and left the room!(What? No good-morning kiss?) Judy returned with a bottle of hospital-grade disinfecting air freshener in each hand and proceeded to saturate the room air with their entire contents! She was accompanied by an aide that cleaned the room and bathroom again and provided us with all new room supplies. Judy kept finding excuses to leave the room, and all I did was repeat my apologies. I was so sick.

The same PT lady I had last seen in recovery appeared with her cheery smile and a walker. She said we would start by moving to the chair across the room and sitting there for a while. Then, if the "explosions" quieted, we would take a walk around the hallways.

Judy stayed and watched and listened to the instruction PT lady shared with us.

I made it to the chair and sat down. It was good to be out of bed. PT lady returned later, and we went for a walk. Once around the nurses' station and back. That walk allowed me to say thanks to all the nurses one more time. I think they were as happy as me that I would be going home. Back to the room, back to the chair. I was tired but happy to be up and about, if only for a short time.

Judy asked if we could take this walker with us and was told we should have been given instructions on how to obtain one. We weren't and wondered, "Now what?"

We had to assure PT lady we would get one, and she cautioned that I would not be able to get from the car to my front door at home without one.

One advantage to living in an "active, over-fifty-five community" is that the neighbors all look out for each other, so we were hopeful someone on the street had a used walker somewhere! Judy contacted a couple of our neighbors and asked if they could call around and find one. She explained that I was "fine" and we would be home in a couple of hours.

A nurse gave me a pill to control the explosions, so it was time to hurry home. I dressed (good-bye, hospital gown), and a nurse came in to remove the last of the IV lines. As one last parting gift, I bled all over the place. The blood thinners worked, and it took a while to get it to stop. Finally, a nice young man with the complimentary mandatory wheelchair arrived to take me to the front door of the hospital.

Judy checked out of the Guest House and brought the car to the hospital door. The nice young man wished us well and helped me lower my pathetic self down and into the low-riding passenger seat. He kept the hospital's walker, and I hoped there would be one waiting for me at home. Judy hit the GPS for directions out of there, and we both prayed the trip home would be uneventful.

The meds they gave me allowed me to sleep most of the way home. I remember it was sunny and warm for an early March Saturday. As we approached the house and parked the car in the driveway, our neighbor Geoff ran across the street to greet us. "You won't believe this. The neighbors brought over four different walkers and two canes!" He continued, "I picked out the tallest walker. It has tennis balls mounted on the front legs so you won't scratch the hardwood floors inside."

Geoff helped get me out of the low-riding car seat and steadied me with the walker before we began to move toward the house, in the front door, and over to my recliner. I was never so happy to sit down and fell asleep almost instantly. I awoke quickly when it became obvious I needed to hurry over to the guest bathroom. Getting me, my surgically repaired leg, drain line, and bag out of my chair and to the walker did not meet the definition of *hurry*.

This would be the first of many hurried trips until my GI tract quieted down over the next couple of days. Poor Judy was there each time. She was worried about me moving too fast and falling, but didn't exactly know what to do. It was the first of many struggles that weekend. I would spend most of my time in the living room reclining chair. Judy devised a folding tray to hold my drink cup and snack tray on my right. The end table to my left would hold my book and the ever important remote control for the TV. (I'm sick, but I can still work the remote!)

I slept each night in my recliner, and Judy insisted on sleeping on the living room sofa next to me. The pain pills provided me with some sleep, but those first few nights, she slept with one eye open making sure "I was fine."

After a nearly a week, I encouraged Judy to return to the comfort of our bedroom so she could get a good night's sleep. It was too soon for me to try the bed because in there, I would roll to one side or the other and that would not be good just yet. I took a full dose of acetaminophen with codeine, and Judy went off to bed. Just after midnight, I learned that maybe it was time to stop with the narcotic-based meds.

To digress for a moment, allow me to describe the rather creepy mailman my neighborhood had when I was very young. Creepy Don delivered to our street every day. He was a tall, thin, older white gentleman with curly silver hair and matching silver glasses. All the children stayed way far away. He was the kind of crabby old guy that they feature in horror movies.

Anyway, I took my meds and went off to dream land, or in this case, nightmare land! Across the room from my recliner was a little alcove that led to our bedroom. There, directly in my line of sight was the door to the linen closet. Sometime after midnight, I suddenly found myself screaming at the top of my lungs. Crazy Don was coming right through the closet door with his arms outstretched and his hands ready to strangle me. It was in full living color—his curly gray hair, his ashen skin, blue uniform, purple shoulder patch, and brown carrier bag. He was out to get *me*!

I began screaming for help and grabbed the handle to allow the recliner to close so I could try to stand. As the footrest of the chair folded, I reached for the walker. Looking down, I suddenly saw a ghostly gown fluttering in front of me on the floor near the walker. "Thom! Thom! WAKEUP! Thom! Thom, you're okay. I'm right here!" Judy was screaming at me to wake up. What I saw on the floor was the bottom edge of her night gown and robe as she hurried to help me. I threw the walker to the side and hugged her and realized it was all a drug-induced nightmare.

Needless to say, that was my last day for acetaminophen with codeine. I began to alternate ibuprofen and acetaminophen for the rest of my recovery.

I slept in my chair for another week, and Judy stayed in bed, but to this day, I still check to be sure that closet door is shut most every night.

CHAPTER FIFTEEN

Ninety-Day Vigilance Begins

So now we take things in ninety-day intervals.
—Dr. Lee Leddy

The sunlight squeezed its way around the living room blinds early Monday morning. It was my first cancer-free Monday, or so I hoped. We would get all the details of where we go from here this morning.

Another trip to Rutledge Tower. This time the parking attendant opened the passenger door and had to retrieve the walker from the backseat, set it up, and help me out of the low-riding car seat. I headed toward the entrance, and Judy hurried in front of me to trigger the automatic swinging door. I shuffled over wondering where she got the energy to hurry.

We walked down the hall and to the elevator. As I looked around, I was reminded that I was in better shape than many others walking with me, and I briefly said thanks to God for getting me this far. If you ever begin to feel sorry for yourself, for any reason, walk the halls of the Rutledge Tower or sit in the lobby at the Hollings Cancer Center. Your afflictions will pale in comparison to many others there.

Up to ortho, into the waiting room, and back to the examination room. This time I sat on the examination table. It would be time to change the dressing again. In walked Dr. Leddy and PA Barrett. "Hey, good morning, how's my team?" Dr. Leddy always makes you feel that you're the only patient he will see today. He's never in a hurry. He's always attentive. You always feel like you're in the right place.

Dr. Leddy started today's conversation with Judy. He wanted to know if *she* was okay. He wanted to hear from her first. He was genuinely concerned. Then he told us that everything looked great. The lab tests would take a while, but he was sure he had clean margins and that all the cancer was removed. Cancer free! Day one!

Then he said as he does now every time, "Okay, let's take a look." Judy knew that for today that was her cue to head out to the hallway and wait. The good doctor said this may be the last time and told me we would remove the dressing long, short, long, and short. Okay, here we go.

"Wow, look at that! The incision site looks absolutely pristine!" I respect a surgeon who admires his own work. He's entitled to be proud; besides, it means I'm in good shape! He inspected the leg in detail and said it looked great and was healing well, the drain line had done its work, and it could go. I did the old deep breath thing, and it was removed before I could exhale all the way. Yuck! Glad that's over.

PA Barrett inspected everything, as did Dr. Duct Tape, who just arrived. They all agreed, so far so good. It worked. So now what? Where do we go from here? I remember asking about a bandage, and he said it wasn't necessary. The incision and drain hole would heal from the inside out over time, and there was no need for any special care for them other than rest and eventually some exercises.

I expressed concern about the odds of it returning to the same place again. Dr. Leddy said it was extremely unlikely. Unlikely, less than a 10 percent chance. Dr. Leddy explained that if this type of cancer was to return, it would most likely do so in the lungs. He went on to share the results of the CT scan done prior to surgery: "Evaluation of the lungs demonstrates stable 4 mm right upper lobe nodule."

He saw the looks on our faces and quickly continued explaining this nodule was so small that if they went in surgically, they may not be able to even find it. It's that small. He said it appeared to be stable and has probably been there for a while. It may be a small scar from an earlier pneumonia or perhaps a tiny, tiny floret of broccoli snorted in long ago. Regardless, we know about it, and it would be monitored. We should return in one week to see how everything is then. The smile on their faces said it all! I was free to go. Free to go home, rest, and recuperate. How do you say thanks for all they've done? How do you say thanks for saving my life? Judy and I both tried, but we said it all with hugs of thanks and left.

By the time we made it down the elevator and into the hospital lobby, I lost it before we got to the door. I sat with Judy and held her hand. I couldn't believe it was over. *Judy was right. I was just fine!*

(I'm gonna be reminded of that for, like, ever!)

The next day, I began walking outside the house. My first adventure was to go to the mailbox at the end of the driveway. Judy opened the door for me and reluctantly allowed me to walk unattended. (I knew she would be watching like a hawk, but I wanted to do this alone.) I went out through the attached garage thinking that I would be alongside the car for part of the time. I emerged from the garage into the warm and wonderful glow of the sun. The air was fresh and clean!

I carefully maneuvered the walker along the driveway, then found myself staring at the drop-off from the driveway to the street. My neighbor Dennis saw my dilemma from across the street and rushed over. "What are you doing out here already?" He quickly took the mail from the box and went to hand it to me. It was then I realized my walker didn't have anything to hold the mail and my hands were tightly wrapped around each grip. Dennis delivered me and the mail back into the house and stayed for a while to visit. I walked each day after that, each day a bit further, sometimes twice a day. I dumped the walker for a pair of crutches by the weekend.

The next time we walked into Rutledge Tower I was cancer-free and on a pair of crutches. I felt great, and Dr. Leddy and PA Barrett said everything looked fine and were pleased with my walking program. He said we could leave now and return in two months for a follow-up appointment. Before then, I should arrange for another

CT of the lungs. If the CT showed no changes, we would then begin routine visits every ninety days. Schedule the CT first, then schedule an appointment with him immediately after. We would then see each other every ninety days for the next two years. *This was the day that we realized that we would now live life in ninety day segments.*

In the weeks that followed, I graduated to just one crutch, and by the return visit in May I was using a cane just to be careful and keep those around me at a safe distance. I had set a goal of six weeks to be back on the bike, but it took me just over two months. The journey was now back where it all began, and I thank God each and every time I ride that bike.

CHAPTER SIXTEEN

Cancer Free: Time to Pay It Forward and Remember Why

The goal is to live a full, productive life even with all that ambiguity. No matter what happens, whether the cancer never flares up again or whether you die, the important thing is that the days that you have had, you will have lived.

—Gilda Radner

As I reflect on the expanse of this journey, it sometimes leaves me breathless and filled with questions. I never said, "Why me?" during all this. Surely, I went through all the stages—denial, anger, bargaining, depression, and acceptance. I did ask a chaplain at MUSC why God left me here. She said I did not have the right to ask that question, and I was not somehow entitled to an answer merely because I survived. She dared me to stay positive and find a way to help other cancer patients, pay it forward, if you will.

Along the way, I talked several times with Ken Burger, a retired *Post and Courier* columnist and author of some feted novels featuring the heritage of Charleston, South Carolina. I had watched at a distance as Ken shared his battle with prostate cancer in his columns long before my journey began. As we talked, he encouraged me to take up a blog or perhaps to write a book about my journey. Ken's own journey ended in the autumn of 2015, but he left behind a legacy of inspiring men to get annual screenings for prostate cancer.

In the middle of my cancer journey, I was fortunate to meet another cancer journeyman, Eric Crawford. Eric quickly became my hero. He was battling osteosarcoma and doing so with unbelievable strength, courage, and determination. Eric and Dr. Leddy introduced me to Swing for the Cure, a fundraising golf tournament for MUSC's sarcoma research. Eric was incredibly intelligent and knew all sorts of statistics about sarcomas, sarcoma research, and sarcomas' rarity and aggressive behaviors. Eric's journey ended far too soon as well. His bravery and determination had an enormous effect on me and everyone he met. One does not forget men like these.

It occurred to me that if God could give me Judy, then send me three angels along my journey to tell me I was fine, then maybe, just maybe, he sent along Ken and Eric to help me recognize why I'm still here. Maybe I need to listen to Ken and tell my story, and maybe I should follow Eric's determination to raise funds and support sarcoma research.

Sarcomas represent just 1 percent of all adult cancer cases diagnosed annually, and 45 percent of those cases occur in limbs, as it did in my case. Sarcomas also account for over 15 percent of all childhood cancers. Over a third of bone sarcomas, like Eric's, and almost a fifth of soft-tissue cancers, like mine, are diagnosed in patients under the age of thirty-five years old.

It is often quoted that one of every six men will develop prostate cancer at some point in their lifetime. Similarly, they say one out of every eight women will develop breast cancer during their lifetime. These cancers seem omnipresent and have often been a rallying cry for raising funds for research.

So if sarcomas are this rare, so too is the funding for their research. One in every one thousand families will have a child with a pediatric sarcoma. One in every one hundred and fifty families will include someone who is battling or has battled with a sarcoma. So maybe sarcomas are not as rare as we thought.

If the story of my journey has made any impression upon you, then perhaps my journey was worth it. I want this writing to bring comfort and guidance to a newly diagnosed sarcoma or other cancer patient. I hope the story of my journey may assist you, a family member or a caregiver, to better prepare for your own journey. Finally, I hope these pages have paid proper tribute to all those who have helped me, cared for me, and quite possibly inspired these humble words to form on these pages.

The sarcoma research done at MUSC may well have saved my life. The treatment plan devised for me was directly influenced by what these doctors learned over time from this research and from brave patients like Ken, Eric, and countless others.

I humbly ask that you consider supporting the valuable, life-saving sarcoma research program at the Medical University of South Carolina by sending your donation to

The Medical University of South Carolina
Sarcoma Research Program
86 Jonathan Lucas Street
MSC 955
Charleston, SC 29425

CONCLUSION

Enjoy the Journey: Smile, Laugh, and Love

The secret of life is enjoying the passage of time.
—James Taylor

If you're reading this conclusion, then my journey reached that seemingly elusive two-year mark—two years post-surgery, two years cancer-free. How many more years are there? Who knows? None of us do. Will the cancer return, or will I have a heart attack and fall over in the front yard? We don't have those answers, and what fun would life be if we did?

I must admit there are some events left out of this text: the phone calls to our sons on the night of the diagnosis; their first visits after they got the news; the sleepless nights; the trips down memory lane together with old photos; e-mails sent bearing our news; and the love, prayers and support returned to us in so very many ways. Every member of Team Positive contributed to this journey greatly. You know who you are, and you have my lifelong love and gratitude.

If you're on your own cancer journey, I hope this text has brought you some insight, some guidance, and perhaps some comfort. Enjoy each day. Laugh often, cry as needed, but laugh more than cry. Surround yourself with your own Team Positive. Do not allow negative people, thoughts, or moods to control you; let them pass and move on. May your good days outnumber the bad. May you rest and heal. May God bless and keep you.

If you are a family member or friend of a cancer patient or someone having any health crisis, just be there. Tell a joke. Share a funny memory from your past. Sneak them a piece of candy. Offer to pray *with* them and pray *for* them each night. Just be there; your presence will bring so much comfort.

If you are a doctor, nurse, caregiver, or researcher, thank you for getting up and going to work each day. May your good days outweigh the bad, and may each day shore up your determination to get up tomorrow and start all over again. Thank you for your compassion, your empathy, and the precious time you spend each day fighting the fight.

There is no magic formula for beating cancer; oh, how we wish for one. There are ways to endure your journey down life's challenging path. Fight like hell; find an advocate to be at your side; build a Team Positive; and surround yourself with warm, funny, positive people and places. Give God thanks for all the days you've had and pray for the strength to enjoy each new day.

Remember those who have fought their fight to completion and have left this earth before us.

Support sarcoma research or the health cause of your choice. Your compassion and generosity will yield hope and healing.

Enjoy the journey. Smile at the sun. Laugh at the rain.

Tell those you love how much you do!

Epilogue I

A Physician's Perspective

by Dr. Lee Leddy, Hollings Cancer Center

Being a surgeon who specializes in oncology is demanding—both physically and emotionally. This is especially true when caring for patients with *rare* cancers. Those patients often feel isolated and frequently have traveled long distances to see providers experienced with rare malignancies. Many patients with cancer present at an advanced stage. This is also true of patients with sarcoma. Those of us who provide care for sarcoma patients are reminded daily of the large gaps in our medical understanding and treatment options for our patients. Simply put, we should be able to do more. I have seen this horrible disease bring out the very best in our species.

What is a sarcoma, and why does it matter? Sarcomas are a rare group of cancers that arise in our connective tissue. They represent 1 percent of all adult cancers and about 15 percent of all pediatric cancers. Given the rarity of these cancers, federal funding agencies often do not direct adequate funds for sarcoma research. It is clear when evaluating survival rates that more research is necessary.

The quest to have an understanding of the basis for diseases and to subsequently discover a cure or to make some small improvement in life of another human is one of the most redeeming characteristics of mankind. To have one's own cells turn against you is something both appalling and disturbing to all of us. We all know someone whose life was invaded by cancer. Many of us know someone who lost their battle with cancer, leaving behind husbands and wives, brothers and sisters, and unfortunately mothers and fathers.

Thom's story is representative of the difficult journey that many adults and children go through. They are poked with needles, poisoned with chemotherapies, burned by radiation, and ultimately cut open to have their pathologic anatomy removed. Some go through this alone; some go through it with an incredible support system. Some survive, and unfortunately some do not. Wouldn't it be great if no one had to go through it at all?

EPILOGUE II

A Spouse's Perspective

by Judy Schmenk

When we received the news that Thom had cancer, my reaction was to be there, strong and positive from the start. That diagnosis comes with a mixed bag of emotions, and instantly I became his caregiver.

Along comes worry. "Would he really be okay?" Somehow all along, I always felt Thom would get through this and regain his normal lifestyle. Nervous tension was palpable every time we went for the scans. There were so many "unknowns" now. What would the bills be like? We heard so many stories of the costs ruining people's lives.

Fortunately, we had a small cancer insurance policy. You know, the kind you pay each month hoping you never need. The coverage was minimal but made the difference to get through financially intact. Dealing with all the insurance companies' claims people and satisfying all their demands seemed to be a trade from anxiety to frustration. We had to check and recheck each statement and fight to correct their "oversights" to pay what they knew they should have all along.

If I were sitting with you now, I would tell you that first and foremost you must be their advocate. Initially, you are both in shock. Then you quickly realize you must be their voice. You have to speak up for *their* needs. You have to ask the hard questions and get all the answers. Keep a diary or have a note pad with you always. Make notes of the questions that come up and then write down what the doctor tells you. Keeping good notes helps take away some of the fear and anxiety. How often we both could not recall what the doctor said just the day before. At least we had the notes to fall back on. It was calming and allowed us to breathe.

As a spouse, friend, caregiver, remember that your health and emotional well-being is important, too. It's not just about the patient—as you are taking that emotional roller-coaster ride right alongside them. Keep your arms and legs inside the car at all times! There will be highs and lows.

Let the patient be themselves. Give them time alone to cope and absorb where they are. One minute you are a cheerleader, the next a shoulder to cry on.

We were fortunate to be surrounded by positive people. There were "our friends," "his friends," and "my friends." They were always there to listen and help. My brother and sister were there to help me vent all my emotions. I am fortunate to still have my mom. I asked her how she handled my father's long battle with cancer and other illnesses. Talking with her was the one place it was okay to cry.

My sons, their wives, and the grandchildren regularly shared their day-to-day news and highlights. Listening to them brought me a sense of normalcy. I could be just Mom or Grandma to them, and I cherished that. Their news, their laughter reminded me that we would all ride out this bump in the road and keep going. As each phone call ended, I realized we raised great kids!

One last thought. Don't be afraid to be a bit selfish. Find a way to pamper yourself and take time just for you. The old saying "You need to take care of yourself first, and then you can care for everyone else" is very true.

My little indulgence was an expensive bath set. The scent lifted my spirits. And I took short walks. These were my moments to breathe and recover.

Our journey through cancer was both similar to many others and yet uniquely our own. Yours will be too.

GLOSSARY

abdomen. The belly area between the chest and pelvis.

ablation. Treatment that destroys very small tumors.

adjuvant therapy. Treatment that is given after the main treatment used to cure the cancer.

allergic reaction. Symptoms caused when the body us trying to rid itself of outside agents.

angiogram. A test that uses x-rays to make pictures of blood flow within an artery.

biopsy. Removal of small amounts of tissue or fluid to be tested for disease.

brachytherapy. Treatment with radioactive objects placed near or in a tumor. Also called internal radiation.

cancer grade. A rating of how cancer cells look like normal cells.

cancer stage. A rating of the growth and spread of cancer.

catheter. A flexible tube inserted in the body to give treatment or drain fluid from the body.

chemoemobilization. Treatment that cuts off blood supply to tumors with beads coated with chemotherapy.

chemoradiation. Treatment with a combination of chemotherapy and radiation.

chemotherapy. Drugs that kill cancer cells by damaging the making of a genetic code.

clinical trial. Research on a test or treatment to assess its safety or how well it works.

computed tomography (CT) scan. Sometimes expressed as CAT scan.

computerized axial tomography (CAT) scan. Uses combination of x-ray images to provide cross section views of a specific are to allow user to see inside without cutting.

contrast. A dye that is put into the body to make clearer pictures during the imaging tests.

core needle biopsy. Removal of a large tissue sample with a thick, hollow needle to test for disease.

deoxyribonucleic acid (DNA). A chain of chemicals inside cells that contains coded instructions for making and controlling cells.

desmoid tumor. A mass of fibrous cells that can grow into nearby tissue but can't spread to distant sites.

embolization. Treatment that cuts of blood supply to tumors with beads inserted into an artery.

endoscopic ultrasound-guided fine needle aspiration (EUS-FNA). Removal of fluid with a needle that is guided with an imaging test to the tumor.

familial adenomatous polyposis (FAP). A health condition that is passed down from parents and increases the chance of getting sarcomas.

external beam radiation therapy (EBRT). Treatment with radiation received from a machine outside the body.

familial adenomatous polyposis (FAP). A health condition passed down from parents and increases the chance of getting sarcoma.

fascia. A deep layer of soft tissue.

fine needle aspiration (FNA). Use of a thin needle to remove fluid or tissue from the body to test for disease.

Gardner's syndrome . A health condition that is passed down from parents and increases the chance of getting sarcoma.

gastroenterologist. A doctor who's an expert in digestive diseases.

gene. A set of coded instructions in cells needed to make new cells and control how cells behave.

general anesthesia. A controlled loss of wakefulness from drugs.

genetic assessment. Testing for diseases that are caused from abnormal information in cells that is passed down from parents.

hereditary. Passed down from parent to child through coded information in cells.

hives. Itchy, swollen and red skin caused by the body trying to rid itself of an outside agent.

imaging. A test that takes pictures of the insides of the body.

immune system. The body's natural defense against disease.

immunotherapy. Treatment that uses the body's natural defense against disease.

intensity-modulated radiation therapy (IMRT). Radiation treatment using small beams of different strengths based on the thickness of the tissue.

interoperative radiation therapy (IORT). Radiation therapy given during surgery.

isolated limb chemotherapy. A method of giving drugs through a needle directly into a leg or arm.

Li-Fraumeni syndrome. A health condition that is passed down from parents that can increase the chance of getting sarcoma.

lymph node. A small group of disease fighting cells.

magnetic resonance imaging (MRI). A test that uses radio waves and powerful magnets to make pictures of the insides of the body.

medical history. All health related events and medications taken to date.

medical oncologist. A doctor who specializes in cancer drugs.

metastasectomy. Surgery to remove tumors that formed far from the first site of cancer.

metastasis. The spread of cancer cells from the first (primary) tumor to a distant site.

mutation. An abnormal change in a cell's coded instructions for making and controlling cells.

neoadjuvant treatment. Treatment given before the main treatment used to cure a disease.

nutritionist. An expert in healthy foods and rink.

observation. A period of testing for cancer growth.

occupational therapist. An expert is helping people regain the skills for management of their health, productivity, and independence in everyday life.

oncology surgeon. A doctor who's an expert in operations that remove cancer.

palliative care. Sometimes called supportive care. Treatment of symptoms of a disease.

pathologist. A doctor who's an expert in testing cells and tissue to find disease.

platelet-derived growth factor receptoralpha polypeptide (PDGFRA). A molecule within a chemical pathway that starts cell growth.

pelvis. The area of the body between the hipbones.

physical exam. A review of the body by a health-care professional for signs of disease.

physical therapist. An expert responsible for management of the patient's movement system.

plain radiograph. A test that uses x-rays to make a picture of the insides of the body.

plastic surgeon. A doctor who's an expert in operations to improve both function and appearance.

positron emission topography (PET). A test that uses radioactive material to see the shape and function of body parts.

primary treatment. The main treatment used to rid the body of cancer.

primary tumor. The first mass of cancer cells to appear in the body.

prognosis. The expected pattern and outcome of a disease based on an exam and tests.

progression. The growth or spread of cancer being tested or treated.

radiation oncologist. A doctor who's an expert in radiation treatment.

radiation therapy. The use of various forms of radiation to treat cancer.

radiologist. A doctor who's an expert in imaging tests.

retroperitoneum. The space in front of the spine and lower trunk.

sarcoma. Cancer that starts in bones or soft tissue of the body.

sedative. A drug that helps a person to relax or go to sleep.

side effect. An unhealthy or unpleasant physical or emotional response to treatment.

simulation. The steps needed to plan and prepare for treatment with radiation.

social worker. An expert in meeting social and emotional needs.

soft-tissue sarcoma. Cancer that starts in tissue that supports, connects, and surrounds parts of your body.

stereostatic body radiation therapy (SBRT). Treatment with radiation that is delivered with precise, high-dose beams.

succinate dehydrogenase (SDH). A protein within cells.

surgery. An operation to remove or repair a part of the body.

surgical margin. The normal-looking tissue around the edge of a tumor that is removed during surgery.

targeted therapy. Treatment with drugs that target a specific or unique feature of cancer cells.

thoracic surgeon. A doctor who's an expert in operations within the chest.

three-dimensional conformal radiation therapy (3D-CRT). Treatment with radiation that uses beams matched to the shape of the tumor.

TP53. An abnormal change in cells that causes Li-Fraumeni syndrome.

ultrasound. A test that uses sound waves to take pictures of the insides of the body.

ABOUT THE AUTHOR

The author spent his youth riding his bike along the shores of Lake Erie in a suburb just east of Cleveland, Ohio. After an injury ended an eighteen-year career in the fire service, he moved with his family to South Carolina. Here, he contributed another eighteen-year career in risk management and insurance.

Just before retiring, Thom returned to his childhood hobby of cycling. It would become a passion and would one day lead to the discovery of a large tumor bulging out of his left hamstring.

After a diagnosis of leiomyosarcoma, Thom shared his plight with a friend, a local Charleston historian and author, who was waging his own fight against prostate cancer. It was Ken Burger's encouragement that got Thom to fulfill a lifelong dream of writing a book.

Thom's wife, Judy, suggested he expand the book to help and encourage others to fight on and persevere in their own cancer fight. "It was cathartic for me," Thom said. "I wanted to tell my story, give hope and comfort to others, and express my gratitude to all the cancer caregivers and researchers who fight this fight every day."

Besides Thom and his wife enjoying his family—his two sons, their wives, and their children — he takes pleasure in swimming, reading, and trips to Lake Lure, North Carolina. He enjoys sharing his story with newly diagnosed cancer patients and working to raise funds for sarcoma research.

CPSIA information can be obtained
at www.ICGtesting.com
Printed in the USA
BVHW030452240621
610314BV00026B/61